S0-AHI-693

WHAT IF You Get Lost?

by Anara Guard

illustrated by Dani Jones

PICTURE WINDOW BOOKS
a capstone imprint

Thanks to our adviser for his expertise and advice:
Terry Flaherty, PhD
Professor of English
Minnesota State University, Mankato

Editor: Shelly Lyons
Designer: Ashlee Suker
Art Director: Nathan Gassman
Production Specialist: Sarah Bennett
The illustrations in this book were created digitally.

Picture Window Books
1710 Roe Crest Drive
North Mankato, MN 56003
877-845-8392
www.capstonepub.com

All books published by Picture Window Books
are manufactured with paper containing at least
10 percent post-consumer waste.

Library of Congress Cataloging-in-Publication Data
Guard, Anara.
 What if you get lost? / by Anara Guard; illustrated by Dani Jones.
   p. cm.– (Danger zone)
Includes index.
 ISBN 978-1-4048-6684-3 (library binding)
 ISBN 978-1-4048-7035-2 (paperback)
1. Safety education–Juvenile literature. 2. Missing
children–Juvenile literature. I. Title. II. Series.
6277998

HQ770.7.G82 2012
613.6083–dc22   2011006549

Printed in the United States of America in North Mankato, Minnesota.
112011   006464R

Has your family ever been lost? Your mom or dad probably asked for help. But what if you get lost by yourself? What would you do? Who could help you?

The stories in this book will show you places you could get lost. They will also tell you who to ask for help.

What If You Are Going to a Busy Place?

José and his family are going to the carnival. Before they arrive, they all put on bright orange shirts. That way it will be easier to find each other in the crowd.

At the park, José's father says, "If you get lost, go to the ticket booth. Tell the person selling tickets that you need help."

They have a great time at the park, and no one gets lost. José is glad he knew what to do.

SAFETY TIP

Make a plan! You and your group can prepare for a trip:

- Wear bright clothing so you stand out in a crowd.
- Pick a meeting place in case anyone gets lost.
- Choose a partner, so you don't go anywhere alone.
- Memorize your parents' names and phone numbers, and your address. Or carry a card in your pocket with this information.

What If You Get Lost on the Way to School?

One day Luis and Jan take a new way to school. Soon nothing looks familiar. Where are they?

Jan asks a mail carrier for help. The mail carrier shows them the way to school.

SAFETY TIP

Stick with what you know!
When an adult isn't with you,
follow a familiar path.

9

What If You Get Lost in a Store?

Rachel plays hide-and-seek in the store.
When she comes out, she can't find her mom.

Rachel is scared. She tells the salesperson
she needs help. Soon they find her mom.

SAFETY TIP

Never hide! Stay near your parents in public places.

What If You Get Lost on a Field Trip?

Evan's class goes to the museum. Evan wants to look at the dinosaur bones for a bit longer. But where did his class go? Who can help Evan?

SAFETY TIP

Stay with your group! On field trips,
it's important to follow the rules
and listen to the adults with you.

13

Evan looks around. He sees people who work at the museum. He asks the guard to help him. The guard finds Evan's teacher.

SAFETY TIP

Look for an adult in uniform! If you get lost in a public place, find someone who works there and ask the person to help you.

What If You Forget Your Way Back?

Meg gathers shells on the beach by herself. Soon she looks up and doesn't see her family.

She finds a mom with children. The woman helps Meg find her mother.

What If You Get Lost in the Woods?

David and his family are camping. He sees a rabbit in the woods and chases it.

Soon David can't see his family's camp area anymore. David is lost, and he's scared.

He remembers his mother telling him to hug a tree if he got lost.

David stays in one place, and soon he hears his parents. He yells to them.

David's parents find him. Now David can hug his mother.

SAFETY TIP

Hug a tree! If you get lost outdoors, stay in one place. Listen for people. Then make noise so they can find you.

Getting lost can be scary. But you can stay safe by following these rules:

- Make a plan! Before going to busy places, make a plan with your group.

- Stick with what you know! When an adult isn't with you, follow a familiar path.

- Never hide! In public places, stay near your parents.

- Stay with your group! On field trips, follow the rules and listen to the adults with you.

- Look for an adult in uniform! When lost, ask for help from someone in charge.

- Never go alone! At new places, never explore alone. If you get lost, you can ask a parent with children for help.

- Hug a tree! If you get lost in the wilderness, stay in one spot and listen for others calling you. Then make noise so they can find you.

Phone Number Fun

In case you get lost, you should know your parents' names and phone numbers, and your address. Here's an easy way to help you learn your phone number:

1 Have an adult help you write down your phone number.

2 Then come up with words that rhyme. For example, if your number is (102) 518-2361, the last number in the area code is 2. A rhyming word is "blue." Another number is 8. "Late" rhymes with 8. Lastly there is a 1. A rhyming word is "fun."

3 Next have an adult help you come up with a song to a familiar tune. It will use your phone number and rhyming words. Here's an example that can be sung to the tune of *Twinkle, Twinkle, Little Star*:

> 102 is sort of blue
> 518 is kind of late
> 2361 wants some fun
> But now it's time our rhyme is done
> 102 and 518
> 2361 now we're done

GLOSSARY

familiar—something or someone you know well

memorize—to learn something in order to remember it always

partner—someone with whom you do something

ticket booth—a place where people buy tickets for an event

uniform—a special set of clothes worn by all of the workers at a place

MORE BOOKS TO READ

Denshire, Jayne. *Safety*. Healthy Habits. Mankato, Minn.: Smart Apple Media, 2011.

Johnson, Jinny. *Being Safe*. Now We Know About. New York: Crabtree Pub. Company, 2010.

Rissman, Rebecca. *We Can Stay Safe*. Chicago: Heinemann Library, 2010.

INTERNET SITES

FactHound offers a safe, fun way to find Internet sites related to this book. All of the sites on FactHound have been researched by our staff.

Here's all you do:

Visit *www.facthound.com*

Type in this code: 9781404866843

Check out projects, games and lots more at
www.capstonekids.com

ABOUT THE AUTHOR

Anara Guard is a short story writer and poet who has worked in the field of injury prevention since 1993. She speaks around the country on a variety of topics related to unintentional and intentional injury. For seven years, she worked for the Children's Safety Network, a national injury and violence prevention resource center. Ms. Guard has also been a parent educator and a librarian. She has a master's degree in library and information science and a certificate in maternal and child health. The mother of two grown sons, she lives and writes in California.

INDEX